TH

of

INCAHOL

& other alcoholic asides

By Aubrey Malone

Published in the UK by
POWERFRESH Limited
Unit 3 Everdon Park
Heartlands Business Park
NN11 8YJ

Telephone   01327 871 777
Facsimile   01327 879 222
E Mail   info@powerfresh.co.uk

Copyright © 2006 Aubrey Malone
Cover and interior layout by Powerfresh
Cover Design Sanjit Saha

ISBN 13: 9781904967576
ISBN 10: 1904967574

Printed in Malta by Gutenberg Press Ltd

A west of Ireland publican was once asked by a tourist what time the pubs closed. 'October,' he was informed.

(Pete McCarthy)

And then there was the drunk who fell outside a pub with a half bottle of whiskey in his back pocket. He panicked when he saw some liquid trickle onto the pavement but then said with a sigh of relief, -Thank God, it's only blood'.

(Jimmy Barley)

A woman drove me to drink and I didn't even have the courtesy to thank her.

(W.C. Fields)

I can't die until the government finds a safe place to bury my liver.

(Phil Harris)

I tried to write a drinking song but I couldn't get past the first few bars.

(Dean Martin)

Please do not leave your seat while the bar is in motion.

(Pub Notice)

Tequila is the gulp of Mexico.

(Sil Fox)

Whiskey makes you see double - and feel single.

(Liza Minnelli)

Excessive drinking causes you to forget three things: names and faces.

(Milton Berle)

Martinis before lunch are like a woman's breasts. One is too many few and three are too many.

(John Humphreys)

I gave up sobriety for Lent.

(Don Rickles)

I drink until I'm drunk. Then I go on drinking until I think I'm sober. Then I know I'm drunk.

(Dean Martin)

A meal without wine is like a day without sunshine, except that on a day without sunshine you can still get drunk.

(Lee Entrekin)

The police said I was drunk but that was an improper diagnosis I Just had a bad reaction to an excess of alcohol.

(Flann O'Brien)

Promises, promises.

(Dorothy Parker after being told by a doctor that she'd be dead in a month if she didn't stop drinking)

I once tried to take my trousers off over my head after a feed of drink. I really thought it was possible. My only worry was how I was going to get them on again.

(Richard Harris)

The Irish have a funny attitude to alcoholism. If somebody tells us they've got cirrhosis of the liver we put out our hand and say Well done'.

(Ardal O'Hanlon)

The jury was unanimous. They sent, out for another barrel of Guinness.

(Niall Toibin)

An alcoholic is a man who drinks more
than you do.

(Dylan Thomas)

An alcoholic is a man who, when he buys
his ties, has to ask if gin makes them run.

(F. Scott Fitzgerald)

Men drink too much for two reasons,
    (a) They're married,
    (b) they're single.

(Ellen Wayne)

Whiskey is the most popular of the cold cure remedies that don't work.

(Leonard Rossiter)

A hangover - the wrath of grapes.

(Jeffrey Barnard)

I've used up all my sick days so now I'm calling in drunk.

(Henny Youngman)

My grandmother is over 80 and still doesn't need glasses. Drinks right out of the bottle.

(Henny Youngman)

Beer-drinking don't'do half the harm of love-making.

(Eden Philpotts)

He has a hole under his nose that all his money goes into.

(Thomas Fuller)

The best temperance lecture 1 ever heard was delivered by a man under the influence of alcohol.

(W.C. Fields)

Do I drink to excess?
I'll drink to anything!

(Errol Flynn)

After I retired I fished and boated a lot, and made Johnny Walker about a quarter of a million dollars richer.

(Dennis Diaz)

I fantasise about whiskey the way other men fantasise about women.

(John B. Keane)

I once became a partner in the wine business, primarily a sleeping, partner. Someone unkindly said I was sometimes more of- a comatose one.

(George Best)

The doctor told me he had some good news and some bad news. The good news was that my liver transplant was going ahead. The bad news was that the donor was Oliver Reed.

(Brian Clough)

The management takes no responsibility for any injuries received in the rush tor the bar at closing time.

(Irish pub notice)

I've only been drunk once in my life - from 1971 to 1990.

(Jim Davison)

I was taking shots for my cold but my wife took the bottle away.

(Rodney Dangerfield)

It's not drinking that causes the hangovers - it's waking up.

(Graffiti)

I spent most of my money on women and booze. The rest I wasted.

(Errol Flynn)

I never need a drink when I drive - only when my wife does.

(Les Dawson)

It's called a 'miniature' cocktail because if you drink one, in a minute you're out.

(Roger Allen)

You can have any drink you like as long as it's whiskey.

(Derek Bates)

To my palate, the sherry tasted like the brine pickled herrings are bottled in, plus a scintilla of dishcloth.

(Kingsley Amis)

I have too much blood in my alcohol stream.

(Dylan Thomas)

I don't have a beer belly. I have a Burgundy belly, it cost me much more money.

(Charles Clarke)

People who go into bars optimistically often come out misty optically.

(Hal Roach)

Work is the curse of the drinking classes.

(Brendan Behan)

I used to gatecrash funerals for free booze. One day a woman found me out and asked me to leave. 'With an attitude like that, I told her, 'you'll never make any friends'.

(Michael Redmond)

Someone told me drinking was slow poison. I replied, "Who's in a hurry?'

(Robert Benchley)

When I don't feel well I drink and when I drink I don't feel well.

(Jackie Gleason)

Sex and a cocktail: they both lasted about as long, had the same effect, and amounted to about the same thing.

(D.H. Lawrence)

What have you been doing in my absinthe?

(Dick Vosburgh)

I have a rare intolerance to herbs, which means I can only drink fermented liquids, such as gin.

(Julie Walters)

The best research for playing a drunk is being a British actor for twenty years.

(Michael Caine)

My main ambition as a gardener is to water my orange trees with gin. Then all I have to do is squeeze the juice into a glass.

(W.C. fields)

I never should have switched from
Scotch to Martini.

*(Humphrey Bogart's
alleged last words)*

A lot of men get very funny about women
drinking. They don't really like it. Well
I'm sorry, lads, but if we didn•t ge? pissed'
most of you would never get shagged.

(Jenny Eclair)

I once saw Michael Scott take alternate sips of Scotch and Akia Seltzer, thereby acquiring and curing a hangover simultaneously.

(Hugh Leonard)

Did you hear about the man who threw a petrol bomb at Alex Higgins He drank it.

(Dennis Taylor)

My favourite drink? The next one.

(George Best)

Drink is our enemy. But the Bible says love your enemies.

(W.C. Fields)

My wife told me it was a disgrace coming home half drunk. 'I know, I said, 'but I ran out of money'.

(Bob Monkhouse)

The only cure for a real hangover is death.

(Robert Benchley)

Pour him outa here.

(Mae West on W.C. Fields)

I used to jog but the ice-cubes kept falling out of my glass.

(David Lee Roth)

The telephone is a good way to talk to people without having to offer them a drink.

(Fran Lebowitz)

I'm allergic to alcohol.
I break out in handcuffs.

(Robert Downey Jr)

I've taken more pledges than drink.

(Brendan Behan)

When I'm playing a drunk I play him as a man trying to be sober instead of a sober man trying to be drunk.

(Michael Caine)

He'll probably never write a good play again.

(George Bernard Shaw on Eugene O'Neill after he gave up alcohol)

I'm not a writer with a drinking problem. I'm a drinker with a writing problem.

(Brendan Behan)

Alcoholics call New Year's Eve
'Amateur Night'.

(Elmore Leonard)

I missed my last AA meeting because I
was too drunk to drive to it.

(Jackie Gleason)

Alex Higgins went to Belfast to launch a ship. The reason, he's not back yet is because he refused to let go of the bottle of champagne.

(Dennis Taylor)

I attended Alcoholics Anonymous for a while. I still drank, but under a different name.

(George Best)

Why do they call it Alcoholics Anonymous when the first thing you say in your speech is 'I'm an alcoholic' - and then give your name?

(Frank Carson)

When I die I want to decompose in a barrel of porter and have it served in all the pubs in Dublin.

(J.P. Donleavy)

One more drink and I'll
be under the host.

(Dorothy Parker)

The insurance company doctor has refused to renew my health policy. The nefarious quack claims he found urine in my whiskey.

(W.C. Fields)

I only drink to make other people seem more interesting.

(George Jean Nathan)

The cocktail party - a device for paying off obligations to people you don't want to invite to dinner.

(Charles Merrill Smith)

Anybody that can't get drunk by midnight ain't trying.

(Toots Shur)

Drunks are rarely amusing unless they know some good songs and lose a lot at poker.

(Karyl Roosevelt)

I'm so holy that when I touch wine, it turns into water.

(John Colville)

Either you're drunk or your braces are lopsided.

(W.C. Fields)

Water taken in moderation
cannot hurt anybody.

(Mark Twain)

I distrust camels, and anyone else who
can go a week without a drink.

(Joe E. Lewis)

My hangover is so bad,
even my hair hurts.

(Milton Berle)

When I played drunks I had to remain
sober because I didn't know how to play
them when I was drunk.

(Richard Burton)

There's nothing wrong with
sobriety in moderation.

(John Ciardi)

I never drink anything stronger
than gin before breakfast.

(W.C. Fields)

The main difference between a drunk and an alcoholic is a drunk doesn't have to attend all those boring old meetings.

(Arthur Lewis)

I don't drink liquor. I don't like it. It makes me feel good.

(Oscar Levant)

Prohibition makes you want to cry into your beer, and denies you the beer to cry into.

(Don Marquis)

An Irish cocktail is half a whiskey with another half added.

(Sean McCann)

Absinthe makes the tart grow fonder.

(Addison Mizner)

Abstinence is the thin end of the pledge.

(Audrey Austin)

I don't spend all my money on drink. I save some for luxuries.

(W.C. Fields)

I drink to forget - but I
can't remember what.

(Henny Youngman)

In God We Trust. All Others Must Pay.

(Pub Notice)

Alcohol is a liquid effective for preserving everything except secrets.

(Henny Youngman)

I'm not a steady drinker - my hand shakes too much.

(Benny Hill)

I'm not drinking any more. But I'm not drinking .any less either.

(Chubby Brown)

Kevin Keegan isn't fit to
lace my whiskies.

(George Best)

I never drink until the children are in bed.
They settle down around 4 pm.

(Phyllis Diller)

A new telephone survey says that 51% of college students drink until they pass out at least once a month. The other 49% didn't answer the phone.

(Craig Kilborn)

Five stages of drunkenness: verbose, jocose, lachrymose bellicose comatose.

(Lucille Heney)

If my hangover isn't too bad I do sit-ups.

(Hugh Grant)

When I was sixteen I walked into a pub.
When I was 45 I walked back out again.

(Ian Pattison)

It's okay for old people to drink really heavily at night because they can go up to bed on that electric chair thing attached to the staircase.

(Rhona Cameron)

I got thrown out of Alcoholics anonymous because when the other guys saw me they thought they were having the DTs.

(Dave Dutton)

I'm not a writer with a drinking problem.
I'm a drinker with a writing problem.

(Brendan Behan)

I'd hate to advocate drugs, alcohol,
violence or insanity, but they've always
worked for me.

(Hunter S. Thompson)

My father was the town drunk. Usually that's not so bad but...New York?

(Henny Youngman)

I was T.T. until Prohibition.

(Groucho Marx)

I only drink moderately. I keep a case of Moderately in my room

(Dean Martin)

The best way to die is to sit under a tree, eat lots of bologna and salami, drink a case of beer, then blow up.

(Art Donovan)

Draft beer, not people.

(Peter Fonda)

Eat, drink and be merry,
for tomorrow ye diet.

(William Gilmour)

Don't tell your troubles to the barman - it may upset his analyst.

(Mort Sahl)

Never wear fly button jeans when you're on a bender

(Spike Milligan)

I bought this tape that you play when you're asleep and it's supposed to stop you drinking. It worked. I don't drink now when I'm asleep.

(George Best)

If you resolve to give up drinking you don't actually live longer; it just seems that way.

(Wilson Mizner)

I'm only a beer teetotaller, not a champagne
one. I don't like beer.

(George Bernard Shaw)

I'm not saying the pub I drink in is rough,
but they have a pig on the counter for an
air freshener.

(Sil Fox)

If I come back in another life, it will be as Richard Harris with a stronger liver.

(Richard Harris)

Archie was having a pint when a fly fell into it. He took it out held it in his hand and said, 'Gae on, ya wee bastart pit it out'.

(Angela Ewen)

Once during Prohibition I was forced to live on nothing but food and water.

(W.C. Fields)

I try not to drink too much because when I drink I bite.

(Bette Midler)

I've only ever been in love with a beer bottle or a mirror.

(Sid Vicious)

I drink too much. The last time I gave a urine sample it had an olive in it.

(Rodney Dangerfield)

I've known banks that give loans to guy who wanted to open bars, and their only collateral was that I was going to drink there.

(Lou Grant)

The doctors have detected some blood in my alcohol stream.

(Dylan Thomas)

When I read how bad drinking was for me
I gave it up. I mean reading.

(Benny Hill)

I spent a large number of my adult years
getting too drunk to remember why I
needed to get drunk.

(Frank Skinner)

I once asked a doctor when he first realised he was an alcoholic. He told me it was when he sprayed vaginal deoderant on a man's face.

(Jeffrey Barnard)

I love to sing and I love to drink scotch, but most people would rather hear me drink scotch.

(G.K. Chesterton)

The chief reason for drinking is the desire to behave in a certain way and then blame it on alcohol.

(Mignon McLaughlin)

A man came to see me this morning absolutely reeking of Horlicks.

(Thomas Beecham)

A man shouldn't fool with booze until he's fifty, and then he's a damn fool if he doesn't.

(William Faulkner)

I saw a notice which said "Drink Canada Dry' - and I've just started.

(Brendan Behan)

There are more old drunkards in the world than old doctors.

(Benjamin Franklin)

There is no hangover on earth like the single malt hangover. It roars in the ears, burns in the stomach and sizzles in the brain like a short circuit. Death is the easy way out.

(lan Bell)

A well-balanced person has a drink in each hand.

(Billy Connolly)

First you take a drink, then the drink takes a drink, then the drink takes you.

(F. Scott Fitzgerald)

Alcohol is a very necessary article. It enables Parliament to do things at eleven at night that no sane person would do at eleven in the morning.

(George Bernard Shaw)

Have I a drinking problem?
Yes - there's never enough!

(Denis Thatcher)

I have made an important medical discovery. Alcohol, taken in sufficient quantities, produces all the effects of intoxication.

(Oscar Wilde)

I always keep a supply of stimulant handy in case I see a snake - which I also keep handy.

(W.C. Fields)

There is no such thing
as a small whiskey.

(Oliver St. John Gogarty)

Please Do Not Ask For Credit As A Kick
In The Face Often Offends.

(Pub Notice)

It's better to drink to forget than
to forget to drink,

(graffiti)

Thou shall not covet thy neighbour's
house unless they have a well-stocked
bar.

(W.C. Fields)

You can't drink all day if you don't start in the morning.

(Les Dawson)

'Never trust a man who doesn't drink' was one of my father's favourite expressions. He died plenty trustworthy.

(Les Patterson)

Boozing with Brendan Behan called for; the thirst of a camel, the stamina of an ox, the stomach of an ostrich...and a neck like a jockey's buttocks.

(Bill Keily)

Teetotalism in an Irishman is unnatural. If unchecked, he becomes unpredictable.

(Hugh Leonard)

I would be happy to see the Devil's buttermilk banned from society,

(Ian Paisley on draught Guinness)

People reckoned I spent all my soccer career in Stringfellows. It wasn't true. I preferred Tramps.

(Charlie Nicholas)

I gave up drinking after realising English became my second language after slurring.

(Billy Connolly)

Right from the start I loved drink, adoring everything about it except the taste.

(Ian Pattison)

I once gave up drinking. It was the worst afternoon of my life.

(Humphrey Bogart)

Some American writers who have known each other for years have never met in the daytime or when both sere sober.

(James Thurber)

By the time I was ten I knew the taste of booze better than tea.

(Brendan Behan)

It's kind of ironic that they tell pregnant women not to drink alcohol in case it harms the baby. If it wasn't for alcohol, most of them wouldn't be that way.

(Rita Rudner)

I always wake up at the crack of ice.

(Joe E. Lewis)

Love makes the world go round? Not at all. Whiskey makes it go round twice as fast.

(Compton MacKenzie)

Wine improves with age. The older I get, the more I like it.

(George Burns)

Owing to the fact that banks have stopped serving alcohol, this establishment will no longer be able to cash cheques.

(Pub notice)

I seldom took a drink on film
sets before 9 a.m.

(W.C Fields)

Avoid hangovers. Stay drunk.

(T-Shirt slogan)

God was an alcoholic. He created the world when he woke up with a hangover.

(Peter Cook)

Colleges are banning alcohol on campus, sending the message to kids, 'If you want to drink, get a car'.

(Will Durst)

Drinking makes such fools of people, and people are such fools to begin with. It compounds a felony.

(Robert Benchley)

Jack London blamed -his excessive drinking on the fact that no nurse was there to keep the liquor from his lips.

(Waldo Frank)

Drunkenness is temporary -suicide.

(Bertrand Russell)

After I made 'The Lost Weekend' I found
myself being looked upon as an authority
on alcoholism. Me, for Christ's sake, a
guy who had to be carted off to bed and
given up for dead if he took three drinks.

(Ray Milland)

At last God caught his eye.

(Harry Secombe's suggested epitaph for a barman)

When an Englishman has a pint too.many he wants to fight or make love or subside into the womb of smutty anecdote. When the Welshman stands behind the bar he wants to sing.

(James Morris)

The main difference between League and Union rugby is that- now I get my hangovers on Monday instead of Sunday.

(Tom David)

I drink to make people bearable.

(Richard Burton)

Some are borns drunks, some achieve drunkenness, but Dylan Thomas liked to have drunkenness thrust upon him.

(Andrew Sinclair)

An Irishman is never drunk as long as he can hold on to a blade of grass and not fall off the face of the earth.

(Joan Larson Kelly)

You're not drunk if you can lie on the floor without holding on.

(Dean Martin)

Once in the Bailey Brendan Behan vomited straight out onto the floor in mid-sentence, but completed it nonetheless.

(John Ryan)

You can order other Little books directly from Powerfresh Limited. All at £2.99 each including postage (UK only)

Postage and packing outside the UK: Europe: add 20% of retail price Rest of the world: add 30% of retail price

To order any Powerfresh book please call 01327 871 777

Powerfresh Limited 3 Everdon Park, Heartlands Business Park, Daventry NN11 8YJ